Winds from Sheol

Winds from Sheol

Fred Phillips

Hippocampus Press
New York

Winds from Sheol © 2017 by Hippocampus Press
Works by Fred Phillips © 2017 Fred Phillips
Introduction © 2017 by Ann K. Schwader

Published by Hippocampus Press
P. O. Box 641, New York, NY 10156.
http://www. hippocampuspress. com

Cover illustration by William Blake, "The Whirlwind of Lovers" (c. 1826).
Cover design by Barbara Briggs Silbert.
Hippocampus Press logo designed by Anastasia Damianakos.

All rights reserved.
No part of this work may be reproduced in any form or by any means
without the written permission of the publisher.

First Edition
1 3 5 7 9 8 6 4 2

ISBN 978-1-61498-207-4

Contents

Introduction, *by Ann K. Schwader*	9
Shadow over Arkham	15
By the Book	16
Song of October	18
Saruman	19
Grandsire's Tomes	20
Jehan	21
Ballade de Guerre Pennsique Troixieme	22
In Elder Days	24
Arboreal Conclave	25
The Worms Forget	26
Cronesong	27
A Dirge at Autumn	28
Fafia	30
The Gathering of the Storm	31
Inn of Memories	32
A Limerick	33
To Serve the King at Gondor	34
A Link	36
Sita of Oudh	38
Myn Lyst	39
The Homeward Pilgrim: A Legend of the Yule	40
Roads	42
A Hand Stronger Than Steel	43
Blade of Barmuzil	45
Persistence	46

Summation	47
Au Revoir	49
An Answer to J. W. Riley's "When the Frost Is on the Pumpkin"	50
Hymn to Thanatos	51
Abandoned Church: Arkham	52
Strangers in a Strange Land	53
Night Hobbies	54
Pay Attention, Jon	55
Eomer's Song	56
The Celeano Fragments, LXII:3	58
Hallowe'en	59
For Permanent Residents of Middle-Earth	60
Autumn Song	62
In the Pavilion of Iskander	63
Guruji Aesclapion	64
The Tale of Muharlal Mun	65
Visitor	66
A Sequel to "Old Christmas" by H. P. Lovecraft	67
The Final Word	70
The Lay of the Last Bard	71
Shadow of the North	73
Faerie Song	74
Conundrum	75
Tribute	76
Legacy of Goldstadt	78
The Ballad of the Snow-Elves	79
Secret Passage	82
Master and Pupil	84
Paean to Duchess Ysabeau	88
Der Brüder Unbekennt	89
There and Home Again	90
Omnes Spectatores Assentiant	92
Judgment	93
Elrond and Celeglas: A Chance Meeting between Two Theoretically Opposed Elvish Heralds	94

Misty Hills	97
Then and Now	98
The Visitors	99
Second Thoughts	100
Homage	101
Tom Byro	102
Poojaree and Sheir-Khan: The Tale of the Priest and the Tiger	103
Many Happy Returns	105
Pivrarcha	106
Rendezvous	107
Hymn to Odin	108
The Song of the Haqqim	109
Reminiscence	111
A Dream of Faerie	112
Orison to Ra	113
Bedmates	114
Reward	115
Meditation	116
Ostrgard	118
The Wanderer's Lay	119
Magister	121
To Jon Singer	122
On Returning from a Pennsic War	123
To Derrick Hussey	124
Frederic the Silent Held in Durance Vile by His Lady	125
Looking Backwards	126
A Maiden's Song	127
The Voyage of Randolph Carter	129
Again a Quest	130
A Song of Fall	131
The Launching of the *Glen Carrig*	132
Dim Horizon	133
From the Uncollected "Tales of an Old Tavern"	134
Solitude	136

Introduction

These are not modern poems. And that is a wonderful thing.

Here, instead, are intricately crafted songs from the long road, full of marvels and experience. Sonnets abound. So do other forms well-suited to the telling of tales, and to the fixing of great deeds and events—real or strikingly imagined—firmly in the mind.

The mythologies of many cultures figure prominently, keeping humanity's first stories alive. Fred Phillips' song-road begins in the depths of ancient Egypt, moving surely from tombs and temples to the haunted wastes of the Red Land. The warrior gods of Scandinavia lend Anglo-Saxon echoes to a few offerings. Eastern tales of djinn and beast recall Kipling. And certain darker mythologies, whispered only by H. P. Lovecraft and his *Weird Tales* compatriots, add their own unabashed pulp flavor.

A considerable stretch of this poet's road winds through the lands of Faerie. Here the memory of J. R. R. Tolkien is honored with remarkable lyricism—and occasional touches of humor, as well. At another bend of the road, Phillips' deep knowledge of medieval history is on full display, as is his bardic experience in the Eastern court of the Society for Creative Anachronism. These last are some of the most elaborate poems in the collection.

There is an unmistakably autumnal tone to these road songs. Halloween and all things October, of course, but also the deeper autumn of a life fully lived and remembered. Occasional poetry is rare today, but such recollections come readily this poet's pen. Many of the choicest are gift-verses to friends (another trait shared with Lovecraft!), and remembrances of fannish gatherings.

Perhaps friendship is what we literary travelers crave most. Well-wrought songs like the ones you'll find here have always been the currency of friendship on the road—and the longer the road, the greater the need.

The winds from Sheol blow for us all, but at least there are delights like these.

ANN K. SCHWADER

Westminster, Colorado
June 2017

To Eugene Martin Souberman

Fons et origo

To get the books
Dost thou conspire,
Yet 'tis in vain
For all thine art,
They quench in me
No raging fire:
Fill not the bookshelf,
But the heart.

Shadow over Arkham

Wait for me, O stranger; pray do not haste—
Quit me not to thy daemonic strand,
Where milestones of grey torchlight grimly stand
To mark unknown and unseen this drear place.
My lores inform me, where there be a Road
There Beings went before. Do not despair,
Therefore, although the shimmering icy air
Hangs heavy here: the gods will bear your load.

I have believed, as many faithful do,
That what the pallid mortal world maligns
As "phantasy" bears truth of elder kind
That, never stated, none the less is true.
So pray, wait for me: be not faint of heart:
Upon this Road the Source of Wonders start.

By the Book

The sixth of January, Ninety-Two,
My wife and I, with naught of note to do,
Flew northward, straight, belike as flieth the Raven,
To Eli's jewel, the city of New Haven.

Thither we ranged, o'er many unknown streets,
Where hidden geas, 'tis writ, and errand meet
Beneath the Gothick battlements and spires
Where youth its hard-won acumen acquires.

Where twenty years hence our distinguished peer,
John Leland, launched his admirable career;
The memories of that day are comfort still
To us, not only that we bought our fill

Of worthy tomes, a Prince's shelves to grace,
But fired our hearts to ever keep that place
Not only ours, but rede for friends to learn
Of that fair city, thither to return.

Exploring all its quaint historic nooks
And browsing through its Fafnir-hoards of books.

With Ninety-Four near gone, to all those here,
List while I send thee cause to shed a tear,
For two full years since wife and I sojourned
To that fair City, for which my heart yearned,

But once alone I visited with friends
Since Ninety-Two—all journeys have their ends,
And ne'ermore since have I dared hope again
To browse New Haven's bookstalls with our friends.

Song of October

In late October, when the daylight fades
At early nightfall when the winds are cold,
And darkness draws its veil o'er copse and glades
While country folk remember tales of old,
Told by their fathers when the world was young,
Of things that throve before the rise of Man
And that are in our festive spirits sung,
And hither leave that they be known again;
We know not whither our feet be led
Unto that destiny our fathers knew;
Thus here we honour living and the dead,
That our own sons may choose the good and true,
The one thing all our lives that we may own—
Fruit from the trees our grandsires had grown.

Saruman

Here in my sturdy keep, bleak Isengard
The wide world in my palantir were caught
Wherewith my secret arts predominate
And order the designs of lesser folk
Unto the reckoning that, to the dark,
May not be stayed from covering the Earth.
Alembics, filled with strange and noxious fumes,
Their deadly reek surrender to the air;
Cracked earthen jugs their mystic burdens hold,
Forsaken by the Ages and the Powers—
Receptacles of Mages' bitterest hopes,
The playthings of an elder, vanished time,
When races vigorously new began
Their rede anent their high and valorous geste;
Fair fountains flowed; fell fires filled far fields;
Great gaunt grey giants gnashèd ghastly gore,
Where mystic Pilgrims came to journey's end;
Our Order that, well schooled in ancient lore,
Was doomed to be the Guardians of the World.

Grandsire's Tomes

It was for this that I was taught to read
From crumbling books my grandsire long had owned
Before I started school. They taught of deeds
No man had done. These tomes were never loaned
But opened only when the moon was full,
And read in silence, as if some dark thing
Its bony hand upon my shoulder pulled
And darkness deeper than the night should bring.
O! books there are a-plenty, and they teach
Of worldly matters, and of common men;
But grandsire's books enjoyed a longer reach—
I do not wish to open them again.
They stand in dusty silence on their shelf—
You would not want to open them yourself!

Jehan

Thy friend was I, when that I served the Crown,
My humble name reflected in thy light,
Nor hath a score of years dimmed thy reknown,
Who ever wert a perfect, gentle knight.
However lavish tourney, game, or feast,
With hope-filled eyes we ever watched for thee,
The Middle's pride, ennobling the dim East,
And e'er a source of comfort wert for me.
Thy epistles keep me ever in thy debt,
For goodness changeth not, nor asketh aught.
Now who will say that we twain were well met
Since I hung up my brand, while still ye fought?
For me, for aye, the measure of a man,
Till that I close my eyes, will be Jehan.

Ballade de Guerre Pennsique Troixieme

NVNCVPATIO DOCTRIBVS IOSEPHVS DE CLASSIS CHAVCERIS MEUM MCMLXXIV

Ful worthie and learned Doctor J., pardie,
A tale I the gyf now, of speres y-brake;
A wel-econtenanced chevauchie—
I wolde nat lett yow whilom that ye spake.

When that the Eastern hoost fared afield,
Mickle sperris and scyldis did they take
For to force the enemie to yield—
I wolde nat lett yow whilom that ye spake.

Ful manie dedys chivauric werre y-dight
That werre wrought all for Chevalerie sake,
Eke faites des coirtesies, eke hem of myght—
I wolde natt let yow whilom that ye spake.

The Kynges Seneschall thre foemen slew
And I slew two ere me dyre Deth did take,
Who then lyved on that mortheknoll were two—
They wold natt let yow whilom that ye spake.

Envoi

Ergo I prythee, Doctor, stand nat still
When angellis unto Petris the do take
Receive remembraunce of thy pupill
Who wold nat lett yow whilom that ye spake.

In Elder Days

Clad in luminescent grey,
Girt with mithril mail,
The High-Elves of the Elder Days
Through the forest steal.
Upon the Vale of Brindumen,
In the twilight's haze,
Before our eyes we see again
The shapes of Elder Days.
Where fall the crystal beads of light,
A rainbow through them plays;
Beneath Lindúmiel, starry-bright
Sprawl walls of Elder Days.
Ah! Fũlthemar, le ainaloth,
The First-Born still hold sway;
Reck surely of a deeper Truth
As in the Elder Days ☩

Arboreal Conclave

Their leader, black as the Pit at Moonset,
His thick caudal appendage astir,
Chittered and clicked till fleeting shadows let
Those nearest him witness his sable fur.
None living know whence his sable clan came,
Or caught a glimpse of him upon the sward,
Each night their cryptic rites were as the same
As human counterparts they wrought toward.
Night drew its ebon veil o'er their disports
That, steeped in dark lore, few could understand;
Black *Sciurius sciuridae* were they, the sorts
That had for aeons lurked upon the land.
In trees they dwell, in darkness hold their rites,
Commanding, not the day, but only night.

The Worms Forget

Before man's foot in Khem first fell
What ruled the two lands none dared tell:
Fell beings of another race
Of which remains no living trace,
And worms before the sun had set
Had no real choice but to forget.

The hawk-faced ruler of the dead
Who governed where the worms were bred,
In whose name was a power reared
That elder deities had feared,
Where now their destiny was met,
The worms would hasten to forget.

Where Djeheuty had taught to write
Sesat, the daughter of the night
In ages lost to human ken
That will not reappear again,
On temple walls still standing yet,
There worms still learn how to forget.

Cronesong

O besom, thou, the only steed I ride
In autumn's chilling wind, to wreak my geste,
While longing for the homely grate inside
My crumbling hovel—tho' 'tis not the best,
Still 'tis my home and hearth to me, where fair
And noble things have truly never been,
So on my spindly steed I sail the air
In homage to our ancient, ragged Queen.
The year 'round men do sleep nights, we allow,
When we from every compass point unite,
The morrow to cast soured milk on cow,
And ruin corn, the which we come to blight,
Ye burn us, yet we bide, thro' foul or fair,
Cast ye a glance behind and we are there.

A Dirge at Autumn

I am not superstitious, I'm as sane as any fan;
I love my meat and drink, and the company of a friend,
But if the lordly pumpkin should slip out of my hand,
Good Lord! You'd think the world at last had come to meet its end. . . .

Ye may tumble leathern pellets down in Mudville's verdant park,
Ye may boot the bouncing spheroid, à la Pele, o'er the ground;
But the grinning global hollow that illuminates the dark
Is the one ball at October's end beside which I'll be found.

When the trees their summer's verdure to the gold of Autumn turn,
When the breathless gasp of August by October's air is saved,
And in millions of front windows the faithful candles burn
In the shells of orange pumpkins each with different features graved.

'Twas my father's portion, Hallowe'en—he was a country lad,
And I a city boy, born and bred, but from his tales I yearn
To learn the lore of field and wood, to savor what he had
When the vine-fruit swells and ripens and the guttering candles burn.

Rockwell paints a moving picture of the simplest autumn leaf
Airborne 'round the hiker's bonnet as he strides along the road,
Which same freedom is denied me and I cannot voice my grief
In a vise of rhyme and metre, nor unburthen here my load.

Once I knew the pine and elder, never hewed the Wise Dam's tree,
And I rambled through the woodlands till my feet were shining red;
But now that all I once loved has been filched away from me—
What have I left to live for? I would just as soon be dead.

Light no candles for me, brethren, ye have known the store I set—
Just a flimsy scrap of paper crowns a lifetime's futile toil,
But in the wind of autumn nights my voice will linger yet,
Crying "Light the fire, sisters mine, and let the cauldron boil!"

Fafia

We wait, with trust unmerited, till Time
With patience clasps us in his weary wings,
Bereft of cause, of reason, or of rhyme,
Enshrouds us as with all material things.
The scenes of childhood with nepenthe lost,
The days with those we ever held as friends,
Like fragile barques upon the tempest tost
All disappear as purple twilight ends.
Nor on our Path are we impelled to turn
To gaze back on the way that we had come,
Although our eyes may mist and hearts may burn,
A fate for all and not for only some.
Despite our station, age, or pelf must go
Each one to where no mortals ever know.

The Gathering of the Storm

The fire burns low, our comrades sleep,
Hilts gripped in hand, our sentries keep
Good watch with one day's battle won—
And yet our work is not yet done.
As we sat at our evening meat
The day would not have seemed complete
Till we had reverenced a king
Our bards have never ceased to sing,
Of steely thews and giant frame
Who never bore a coward's shame.
The mists of memory revealed
A figure legend had concealed
What race from darkness had assigned
A monarch of a different kind.
Our kingdom would not be today
A realm where children safely play,
If with his sword he had not shown
What one man could achieve alone.
Hail, chieftain, hero of our lore—
May our swords be forever yours!

Inn of Memories

"Put thy load down, Gaffer, and rest thy feet,"
  The landlord quoth. The old man dropped his pack,
  Called for a pint, then stretched and leaned well back.
'Twas not an inn of fashion, yet 'twas meet
  For wanderers who trod those paths not sought
  By Everyman o'er leas where once were found
  Fell warriors, iron-clad, who stained the ground
  And reaped the victories their preuesse bought.
  None thither knew this ancient, greying man
  Who his own counsel kept, yet with a mien
  That none of living men had ever seen
  Ere since the weary, woeful world began.
  He donned his pack, its straps he fastened tight,
  Arose and disappeared into the night.

A Limerick

A shoggoth from unknown dimension
Sought ways of relieving its tension.
It materialized
In invisible skies
In a way too hideous to mention.

To Serve the King at Gondor

Behold the peasant of Bretonnie,
All armed cap-a-pie is he,
A strides the pike full merrilie
To serve the King of Gondor.

And here a pikeman Allemayne,
His cap were short, his hose were pleyn,
A marcheth in a driving reyn
To serve the King at Gondor.

And lo! a lad of Lombardie,
But sixteen summers' worth hath he,
Yet beareth shield full royallie,
To serve the King at Gondor.

The English yeoman loves the chase;
From ringing steel he turns his face;
Now England's shame and God's disgrace
Serves not the King of Gondor.

Ye soldiers all from evrie clyme,
Behold! it is the fightyng tyme;
Who would be sung a hero's rhyme,
Come serve the King at Gondor.

A Link

I seal forever in these asphalt streets
Whatever hope of Romance I would meet;
If secrets hide here, long have they been still
And here there floats no song of whippoorwill,
But only raucous engines, day and night,
Which long ago the Pixies put to flight.
See manifest about us works of Man
Who seeks credit what someone else began,
And pity those of us who know the Way
That was begun in some lost bygone day;
For albeit the Road goes ever on,
The feet of millions have so tramped upon
Its weathered pavestones, one can scarce recall
That ever there was here a Road at all.
But he is not a hunter who would lose
That scent of hazard that were his to choose.
I call not on their Names who went before;
Let gods who sleep alone: what would ye more?
But that Spirit that would serve Them still
I summon forth again with royal will.
'Tis possible They respect the kind of blade

Who seeks his quest and calls not Them to aid,
And now remember well the words of yore
Which ye have somewhere, sometime read before:

"Bule imbe risarant; bele imbe echarant; tan imbe bytlarant;
mer (hain) alem utari."

(Deep they delved us, fair they wrought us, high they builded us,
but they're gone.)

Sita of Oudh

She comes, not in palanquin rich with gold,
Or in the howdah of a Rajah's chair,
But sits a steed, as Ranis did of old,
With adamant asparkle in her hair.
No train of slaves attended her in state,
No host by her preuesse hath e'er been broke;
And yet she sits among the Good and Great
And governs, like Dentatus,* noble folk.
Her heart is humble, but her words are wise,
She heals what baser hands would rend apart,
And truth may e'er be witnessed in her eyes,
Those lamps of light that shew her truest heart.
She must not weep, this Deva Das† divine—
O, Sita, Maha Jani, we are thine!

—Frederic the Silent, C. S. C.
XX Jan. MCMLXXV, A. S. IX
God save the King!

*M. Curius Dentatus, a Senator of the Republic, who sent away ambassadors who tried to bribe him with richly chased silver bowls, saying, "I had rather command those who live in plenty while I continue in poverty."
†Deva Das—slave girl of the Gods

Myn Lyst

I am a trewe clerke who bokes seeketh
Myn shelfes with theyr tytles waxen fat;
Alway of bokes-hunt am I spekyng
Qui exquireit, reperiat.
God sende me peas, to ye worthie ende
The wallys of myn hous brast nat asunder,
And yeve me that myn lyst may somedel mend
The whylk schal mickel of myn gossips maken wondre.

The Homeward Pilgrim:
A Legend of the Yule

Come, brethren, merry at feast, who love to hear me tell,
At Yuletide season's holy peace, of them who used to dwell
Among the ancients of our race, and hear their gestes withal
That some small comfort prove to-night within our festive hall.

'Twas in the reign of Henry, forbear of the Lion-Heart,
That from the shores of Merry England pilgrimage would start
And three years Outremer Winifred of St. Mark
Heard lapping wave and raucous knave, and yeoman's brachets bark.

Philistia's sandy soil felt well the imprint of his tread.
He shrove himself at holy shrines; did reverence to the dead;
And finally Holy Sepulchre lay quiet 'neath his view,
And homeward turn'd his footsteps, as palmers are wont to do.

Through Phrygia and Stygia, Winifred trod the dusty road,
And knelt each night in prayer as he rested him his load,
For a sinner's burthens weigh him down far heavier than lead,
And the good life is the only means by which this load be shed. . . .

And when at last he came upon the land that he had known,
None bided thither from among the folk who were his own,

With empty heart he laid his staff upon the English soil,
And pondered long what Time had wrought to make him such a coil.

To all then who will hope to fare abroad to distant lands
And spill their blood and tears upon uncomprehending sands,
We speak most sombre orisons that they may wisely wait
And spare themselves the dolour of our Winifred's estate.

Roads

The track to ancient Samarkand were long
And wound o'er all the features of the Earth;
Bones by its wayside bleached, the prey of strong
Indomitable warriors, and their worth
Hath reached and fed the heart that drives this quill . . .
O, Roads! The sea-wolves' way were ne'er so dark,
Nor weed-grown tracks that through dark forests spill
Compared to those o'er which my letters hark
From our old friend scant answer—though the ground,
Bestrewn with crispèd leaves, to frost adheres.
Each season tells, its course rolled duly round,
A tale of lengthy months and lonely years,
And we must learn our lots (as well we know)
O'er different Roads, as we were meant to go . . .

A Hand Stronger Than Steel

The moon was pale as Almain steel
As daemon-voices howled;
A horde of red-eyed monsters quailed
Before a warrior cowled;
His bright blade rose like a wind of snows
As a strident voice he raised:
"Who will first feel my edge of steel
And end his hellish days?"
The rout of knaves for booty craved
And roundly cursed their prey,
But with a yell his sword-arm fell,
And blood began to spray.
"Come forth, ye swine—thy lives are mine;
In red coin will I pay—
Who seeks to loot my metal suit
Must earn his keep today!"
The dastards paused, his swordplay caused
More than a few to fall.
"Give way!" one cried. "His sword is tried,
We need not perish all!"
They backed away in disarray,
And one by one they fled.

"Small profit we shall this night see,"
    Abandoning their dead.
The warrior's blade in sheath he laid,
    His preuesse not in vain,
And breathed a word—"Beware my sword,
    If ye dare come again!"

Blade of Barmuzil

Who ken but that Telerion, the last
Prince of the Late-Comers, of all his kin,
Ward of annals of his lustrous kin,
Should o'er distant lands rove, and hold within
His noble bosom rede of ages lost
Deep in the mists of Time, known but to one
Among the Bars of lands lost in the past
To when the tale of his kin was begun.
At Barmuzil when fearsome hosts by night
And day in iron grip fought unto death
And left its ancient walls a crumbled sight,
The final end to which his footsteps led,
Thus let for sake of honour fall a tear
On Prince Telerion his final bier.

Persistence

How oft have we this Dragon wholly slain
By God's command, and bore his fiery breath;
And yet this chronic Beast must rise again,
To mark the boundary of life and death?
On all the world his sombre shadow falls:
What son of Adam safe within his sight,
Behind the most impervious of walls?
His darkness is the enemy of light,
And when our day is fled, our sons will stand
Against the fearful compass of his wings,
Unless an angel reaches for our hand
And lends us hope of more eternal things.
Although the Dragon we may never slay,
We will not follow those who run away.

Summation

You may with justice say to me
I am not all I ought to be;
I own no home and no garage,
My bank account is not that large.
When Winter comes, the Virgin Isles
Are not what you would call my style.
Instead I stroll in Central Park
Before the sky becomes too dark,
Where all the people long have fled
To fire and meat, and lamp and bed,
And trudge there through the silent snow
To where Snow Elves are wont to go,
And you can find me standing there
And breathing vapour in the air,
Regarding branches traced in ice;
For me such crystal webs suffice.
I need no Jags or limousines
Nor Southern France's lavish scenes;
I would not take your jai-alai
For swirling flakes in a winter sky

That past the golden streetlamps fall
And with their mantle over all . . .
And so if I'm not what might be
I am no less than what you see . . .
A city-boy from northern clime
Who dearly loves the winter-time.

Au Revoir

The Sphynx o'er endless vistas holds her gaze
And future fate divineth for our quest,
But e'en the Wise cannot foretell all days,
And we, ourselves, can only do our best.
Thus whether we shall meet upon this strand
Or in a better place, nor you, nor we
For all our learnèd counsels understand,
Since Seigneur Dieu alone knows what may be.
So first come take a glass and then our hand
And take a little piece of every heart;
Remember always our hard-working band,
And know that all must end that ever starts.
So think of us where you bide, near or far,
Say not "adieu" but only "au revoir."

An Answer to J. W. Riley's "When the Frost Is on the Pumpkin"

When the dew is on the medder an' the sun is hardly riz,
An' the gloomy sky at nighttime gits to be as dark as is,
'Fore the kettle starts a-bubblin' an' the biscuits ain't yet browned,
An' a feller ain't got up yet from the place where he lay down,
O, it's time to be a-thinkin' of how good it is to share
Early sunlight for his chores an' the clean, fresh mornin' air,
An' of all his daily blessins, when he comes to take their stock,
When the frost is on the punkin an' the fodder's in the shock.

Hymn to Thanatos

Pray that I may die and put this pen
To rest, that it may trouble me no more;
Thus have I prayed and wept, though all in vain:
God shields no sinners, howso they implore.
And who maintains we only think of Death
When we are ill, nor welcome would it be
If it appeared, to catch our final breath
And lead our feet toward Eternity,
Persists in error, for such is our woe
That Death would come as friend, nor be despised.
For Man hath but a little way to go
Ere that of his last geste he be emprised.
So welcome, gentle Death; we need not fear
Our mortal failings, now that Death is here.

Abandoned Church: Arkham

The traves, the clerestory, filled with the fumes
Of sanctity that defy the hopeless night,
Mute testimony of a hope that might,
One golden day, walk in these very rooms,

Even on Arkham's aged, greying street
This quiet place reposes, deaf to power
That claims for its own guerdon, midnight hour
Where apparitions pent in madness meet.
Few pass here where unknown feet have trod
And left desperate prayers unto their god.

Strangers in a Strange Land

In Khem we wandered, hours ere Ra his face
Showed to the world in summer's febrile glare,
For we had traveled from a temperate place
To tread the sands that knew our footfall there.
And every day I asked, "What drew me here
In August, to the world where Time began?
And surreptitiously I dried my tears
While trudging through the world of Early Man.
I yearned for home, my heart was not content
In tomb, in mosque and palace, and I yearned
By bringing me to where the Heavens burned
The ajnabi,* Franjid† who had fled
A cooler land, to walk among the dead.

*foreigner
†European, Westerner

Night Hobbies

Fell the blast of winter's voices, as the King of Frost rejoices,
And the street-lamps dimly flicker in a world of twinkling white;
Over rooftops drifts are piling and the daemon-faces smiling,
For at last they are the undisputed Masters of the Night.

And while Stygian silence reigns behind the darkened windowpanes,
Not even squeaking waggon-wheels to cheer the frozen gloom,
Here my flickering candles gutter with their sibiliating stutter,
While I settle down to Lovecraft in my dusty attic room.

Through the roof-boards, all a-kilter, tiny streams of powder filter,
And the numbness in my hands gives way to Arkham's spell,
To the plaintive wail of sorrow; Devil take the mundane morrow,
Which I dread with terror deeper than the fear of hell.

For tomorrow this will vanish, and the business world will banish
HPL to all the dreadful regions of Ethereal Man,
But while Arkham's Silent People congregate beneath their steeple,
Let the howling winds complain, but I'll read Lovecraft while I can.

Pay Attention, Jon

Long fled those happy days of yesteryear
When vanished bretheren ranged around the fire,
Each fortified by punch, or wine, or beer
And able to find naught more to desire.
Fell winter's dread was thus kept well at bay,
And songs we used to sing gave all high cheer;
How different is our lot become today,
Without a single comrade dwelling near.
Our first toast, with unmelted snow on cap,
"To absent friends" we raised, and to the hour
When from all points of the familiar map,
And sweetened lives, lest they grow sour.
O! All my unspent days would I amend
If I might only have my friends again.

Eomer's Song

Where is the horse and the rider in the red dawn breaking?
Where is the horn gold-carved, the shied-bearer waking?
Who shall pour the mead and bring forth the ancient sword?
Who shall mount the guard and keep oaths to his lord?
Dire is the need by night, by day the terror growing;
Out of the East rolls Shadow, and cruel winds blowing;
Fire and fear upon us and doom swiftly flying—
Who shall stand with the living and avenge the dying?
Where is the banner of old that our Kings fought under?
Where is the clash of the shields and the hooves like thunder?
Where is the column of men, like forked lightning,
That rode down from the North, in the dawn brightening?
Hail to the blood of the ancients in our veins flowing,
Honour the wisdom guarded by our Elders knowing;
Swiftly the years fall on us, like foes without number—
Too soon the last sortie and the Long Slumber.
Where are the lips that kissed us, our foot in the stirrup waiting,
Where is our joy of battle, and our teeth grating;
Where are our comrades faithful in their steel shining,
Where is the brawny berserker, for slaughter pining?

Let the eoreds assemble, let hands grip spear;
Pull tight the straps of your shields, and banish fear;
We ride like our fathers of old to whatever the day may bring—
Westu Theoden hal! Hail, Theoden King!

The Celeano Fragments, LXII:3

Behold the Shambler from the Stars!
The Evil One is but a servant of His servants,
Nor hath the Lord God over Him any dominion;
Universes uncounted roll in the Chaos of His abysmal maw;
Woe to thee, O Jerusalem; abandon hope, O Zion,
For the Reckoning of the Ages is upon us,
Neither may the righteous nor the iniquitous escape His toils;
Eternity is His footstall, Infinity his handmaiden,
And the end of all that is, is come . . .

> As annotated in the Pnakotic
> Manuscripts, tr. Prof. Josiah Ralston,
> Miskatonic University Press, 1927

Hallowe'en

October's diachromic leaves are spent
In winds a gamut run from mild to cold,
Until the sixteenth day of Scorpio bent
Their gaudy branches prematurely old.
Fell wraiths in leaf-smoke surreptitious form
And eldritch shadows over Luna soar;
The hearth grows cozy in the autumn morn,
And summer's zephyrs rustle leaves no more.
The days are shrunk; the byre and barn are full;
Both man and kine fell winter face replete.
How strange a force upon our spirits pulls,
From cold—or fear—to shiver, 'tis but meet.
Whereso ye go, wherever you have been,
Both dead and living share the Hallowe'en.

For Permanent Residents of Middle-Earth

In the toils of the steel-clad city, where we sweat for our daily bread,
And we long for the shadows of evening—fire, lamp, meat, and bed,
In the bellies of metal-wheeled dragons, jammed in like the gold of a hoard,
We long for the fields of Tasarinen, where freedom was bought with a sword.

Ah! Then, O my masters and lovers, a life was not reckoned in gold,
One might trail a pike or delve the earth until one was bent and old,
And the air was sweet, and a candle's light gave comfort, peace, and aid,
One might dwell with hope by the roadside, and never be afraid.

And the Elves were not merely a legend, but they lived and had commerce with men—
Great God! but I'd give my life and wealth to bring them back again!
And the Dwarves came above ground and traded, the Masters of their craft,
And the Elves lit the forest with Music, and they sang, made merry, and laughed.

And the earth was young in its greenness, and the dew lay like pearls on the grass,

There were wars, too! Aye, there was honour—but it was too good to
 last;
We have come to a new Age of Darkness—the Dark Tower is builded
 anew,
They have only scotch'd Sauron, not killed him—now the rest is up to
 you.

Take down from the wall thy father's sword, but draw it only at need;
Take down from the mantle thy gran'ther's harp that sang many a
 glorious deed,
O, the Road is still there that they traveled, the Nine Companions of
 old—
Ye may set out a-questing upon it, for the trail has never grown cold.

And if, as Fate would have it, ye should meet others of your kind
At the Sign of the Prancing Pony, where the roads in the darkness wind,
Take a pint if ye miss me at gloaming, for I'll soon be following,
And keep mindful the rede of the Old One—and do not put on that
 Ring!

Autumn Song

A single leaf does not attract the eye,
But when a thousand of them fill the sky,
All know that summer's course at last is run
And golden autumn's glorious reign begun.
The verdant fields abound with luscious fruit,
And fleeting game do hunters stalk to shoot;
The rafters of the goodman's cottage weigh
With loops of sausage, and each passing day
Brings deeper chill until the corn he reaps
Into the bulging silo heaves and keeps
Against the winter, hard on autumn's heels,
And snugly round the blazing fire they feel.
O come, Queen of the Year, in high array,
The other seasons' homage thee to pay.

In the Pavilion of Iskander

Go, Neocras, bring the lamp
And to thou, Aristomachos, cast thy holy runes
That we may know what the Gods ordain.
Thus: the cast of Krylon;
Patipater—where is that lazy boy?
Get out from under there, you scoundrel
I don't care what he promised you.
Go and hone my sword to a fine edge.
Do not heed this baggage. Aristomachos
For a Thracian, you are a clever fellow—
Try again. So! The cast of Medusa!
Archistarchus, get your stylus
And write what I shall say to you.
"Dear Uncle, May the Gods preserve you.
I will not be home for the Feast of Phallos.
Send my scrolls to Megistopolis,
and don't go near the porter."
Οἱ vῆί!

Guruji Aesclapion

From land afar in legends aeons lost
Where men and godlings frequent commerce knew,
There gurus dwelt, no more sagacious host
From Sakti sprung in sunlight and in dew
And ministered unto the need of man
In seemly measure easing him of pain,
Yet none knew whence or whether they began
Or whether they would leave their mark again.
Poor poets sing their paeans to the wise,
Their deeds on stones for aeons graven deep,
And echoes of their passing through the skies
Keep ward on men in waking and in sleep.
Show us thy favour, Children of the Night,
And from our darkness, lead us to the light.

The Tale of Muharlal Mun

O'er the Tupal Close the biting snows
Blow fierce on the plains of Hind;
From Kalprapur to Ranjipur
There thunders an icy wind.

And caravans wait by Khyber's Gate
Till Nature its course hath run;
Let my Masters hear with willing ear
The fate of Muharlal Mun.

'Twas ill design urged him to climb
To a shrine of forgotten years,
That to gods unknown to few alone
Had blood and labour reared.

And thither he cried to Those Outside
His life and service swore,
Nor was Muharlal Mun his office done
To Them who came before.

And to this day from distant ways
A dread yet has not done
In holding sway both night and day
O'er the Shrine of Muharlal Mun.

Visitor

When darkness over Bekra drew its veil
Some movement was discerned that had not been
By any living being ever seen
Or rendered in some long-forgotten tale.
A shape, man-like, its shadow slowly strayed
Far darker than the living night could hold—
A presence that would terrify the bold
To wreak whatso a higher Power bade.
The market in its ancient timeless square,
Once Ra again unveiled His shining face,
Was not what had once been a crowded place,
But of men's footfall curiously bare;
And Bekra to which once was commerce led
Is no more than a city of the dead.

A Sequel to "Old Christmas" by H. P. Lovecraft

There used to be on Yules of recent years
A place to which First Saturdays were steered;
Ye fans of recent whiles, now heed our song
Whose tidings we will not make overlong,
Detaining you from more intriguing games
Whilst we recall the stately Yule-log flames
At one remove, the which were wont to sing
The fans of yesterday while reveling
At the most blessed mirthful time of year
When even fans are called to make good cheer
And stay their mocking, while for one sweet night
They fared forth with their songs and bore their lights.
The Pierian Muse evoked beneath their sills
As though all heedless of December's chills.
Our learned doctor led the company forth
Now pushed, now pulled by winds down from the north,
Betimes through snowless streets, or lashed with rain,
Albeit scarce one reveler would complain.
While flushed with energy, our happy throng
With merry will would raise its voice in song.

The last time carolers thus trooped the streets,
Our worthy yearly host led forth our feet
To where one H. P. Lovecraft used to dwell,
And thither, frozen, 'neath his window-sill,
We chanted, ere the custom disappeared
The lay, "It Came Upon a Midnight Clear."
We came at length to one Italian house
Within which forty kinsmen made carouse,
And round their piano with their children raised
Our voice in "Jingle Bells." Those sprightly days,
Their echoes faded, linger in our song
Where happier customs do by right belong.
And when our faces, red as cherries, we
Our singing done, turned homewards eagerly,
And through the door we trudged in, bluff and hale,
A thousand cooking-smells each nose assailed,
And saw, where jigsaw puzzles now hold sway,
A Groaning Board to crown the festive day.
No Jotunheimer could, from first to last,
Work through that massive feast to break his fast.
The doctor's lady, with their friends' support,

Had cooked and roasted viands of each sort
From bouillabaisse to chestnuts, there to feed
Our stalwart company for its tuneful deeds.
Alas! from whatsoever cause no more
Do fans go forth as once we did of yore
And fill with song the silent wintry streets
As once the Yuletide we were wont to greet;
For like the leaves of autumn, our old band
Has blown to distant corners of the land
And only here, in our poor song recall
The ebullient spirit of that seasons' hall.
For we lack skill to make such glee survive
And bring the joys of Yule once more alive;
To drive grey skies away we lack the tools
That we, as fans, might know the grace of Yule.

The Final Word

I may not plough the seas or hold a breach,
Or march with banners in a battle-line;
I may not learn the wisdom that they teach
In ivied halls where centuries combine;
I may not visit sanctuaried shrines,
Nor fill the aching void within, to know
The myriad of the Maker's grand designs,
Nor where the iridescent rainbows go;
I may not speak, or hear the lowing herd,
Or take the ease with friends my labours earn
That has for ages salved, with gentle word,
The world's afflictions when they maim and burn.
I may not tread the earth, nor see the sky,
But hither must I weaken, sink, and die.

The Lay of the Last Bard

Let the shades of the Bardic dead cry their lament,
Let Taillefer juggle his brand;
Let a pall in the hall fall on those, pleasure-bent,
Who despite Bardic art out-of-hand.

No more shall the tale of the hero redound
In the words of the passionate skald;
After meat, who will ever again gather 'round
To brighten with song the great hall?

They are done, who with nobles and prelates remould
All the romance of Chivalric deeds;
Even great oaks must bend with the storm, it is told,
And the future will know only weeds!

In the days when our monarchs were new to the throne,
There were few Bards to sing of their geste;
But now that the number of singers has grown,
They are lumped in the rear with the rest.

I will wager my beard that the art of the poet
Will never win proper renown,
Nor will guests in our hall hear scarcely a note
With loud-mouthed louts shouting them down!

The voice of the singer is silenced for aye,
The time of his glory is passed;
No more shall his strains of song mount to the sky,
For this lay that we sing is the last!

Yet some morning afar-off in some distant time,
A Bard of the future shall weep,
And lament at the meagreness of his own rhyme,
While the dead singers groan in their sleep.

"O, ye men of the past, wherefore drowned ye our song?
Sure, the evil ye wrought us were hard;
For life is but fleeting, and death were too long
To restore us the voice of the Bard!"

Shadow of the North

The stolid granite hills are still as bleak
As when he climbed them centuries ago
In northern lands, unfitted for the weak
Where grasses withered 'neath the sweeping snow.
Thither he life's harshest lessons learned;
Though afterward high crowns became his meed,
He wandered where the desert wastelands burned,
A cold grey wife his comfort and his creed.
Above his rock-hewn tomb the winds are cold,
And where his sword reposes, no man knows;
The rune-carved rocks above his bier have told
The tale that led him to his last repose,
And when, down from the North, the night winds blow,
The tribesmen sing his tales of long ago.

Faerie Song

Soft the sound of summer lingers
In the night's enchanted air,
Far from Aurora's rosy fingers
In a stillness bright and fair.
Crickets far from hearthside creaking;
Glowworms now—or are they Elves?
Quiet faerie-rings are seeking,
Singing softly to themselves.
Do thou place, O Child of Twilight,
This my scrivening next thy heart;
As I peer out through the skylight,
Grieving o'er my finished part,
And e'er will I bear with me
Clear remembrance of thee.

Conundrum

Why do the dwellers on our planet need
To risk annihilation of their race,
When beings from the furthest depths of space
So gloatingly upon their conflict feed?
We were not first, though we may be the last
Upon our swirling orb in space to dwell;
'Twas writ, from heaven can be made a hell,
And hell a heaven: trust we not that hour
As needed to preserve our form of life
Instead of preying in an endless strife
The while blasphemous beings stay their power
And wait till we annihilate our race,
And leave them undisputed lord of space?

Tribute

Pale in their hands, the weathered caskets bear
The gems, each worth the ransom of a king;
Before them, lords of long repute compare
The fabled treasures that their minions bring
And heap before the Spectre's bony feet
And cling about his knees, there to entreat:

"O, grimmest Scytheman, loose thou from thy thrall
These shining faces, lately flushed with youth,
And let them now depart thy gloomy hall,
For they have paid the price to learn the Truth.
We will surrender greater gifts than these
If thy inexorable hold will cease."

No answer makes the Shade. The voices rise;
The wails grow plaintive; cheeks are drenched with tears,
And from their midst a groan lifts to the skies
From which no succour finally appears.
The pile of tribute grows, its wealth abounds,
With jeweled brands and gem-encrusted crowns.

The conqueror lies prostrate and bemoans
The price his triumphs cost him thousandfold,

Who now must reck the value of his Throne
In living men who may not be recalled;
And he must pay, whose soul dwells in his sword,
That price no living human can afford.

And they will weep in vain, who thus engage
(Nor ever, once they close, will ope those Gates)
To parley with their silver tongues, or rage—
Who hopes for mercy, he forever waits,
And to his grisly list of guests adds more,
While stubborn men insist on waging war.

Legacy of Goldstadt

'Twas not with magick means with which I raised it,
But Aesculapian lore learned at great cost,
And now I rue the day my soul was lost
In such wise the world at large appraised it.
Can Man tread on the steps of the Creator
The mysteries of life and death to wield?
I rue me that Fate dragged me to that field,
In lieu of wholesome texts I might use later.
Must Nature's awesome secrets be appraised?
Must Man her knowledge Nature then compel
That could make of his dream of heaven hell,
And pow'rs that should be dormant then be raised?
I rue me that the truth came to me late
And my name blackened with a sinful Fate.

The Ballad of the Snow-Elves

There was in Outremer a Knight
Lay dying on the sand,
And heavy woe did him bedight
To die in foreign land.

For he had smote the livelong day
As chroniclers well know,
And he was chiefest in the fray
Ere that they laid him low.

And these words spake ere that the breath
Did utterly from him spend:
"O God, I would a cooler death
When that I meet my end.

"The sky here pity knoweth not,
And slays us every day,
For this were devilish and hot
A price for Christ to pay.

"But I remember me of old
In England whence I came,
'Twas merry work to brave the cold
When battle was the game.

"And I remember many a watch
 I kept with cloudy breath
 Betwixt the vigours of our march
 That led to fame or death.

"The ferlie creatures of the night
 Were mickle as the leaves
 That waved on boughs from left to right
 And fell by twos and threes.

"And in November's latter part
 When these by wind were tost,
 King Winter's van would grimly start
 To lead his frozen host.

"And silver traces on their veins
 From green to red and gold
 The Snow-Elves drave their dainty wains
 And never felt the cold."

And now the Knight his bosom heaved,
And quoth, "Jesu, mercy,
For in Thee I have well believed
And find new life in Thee."

So send we from this festive hall
To our brothers far away,
That they be gathered one and all
To where Snow-Elves hold sway.

> Feolildwyniensis +++
> Baron Frederic of Feolildwyn, CSC, PMC
> xxix Novembris MCMLXXVII. A. S. XIII
> God Save the King!

Secret Passage

But press a quarter of this shield of stone,
Good mistress, and this block will roll aside;
Then pull this ring and chain—we're quite alone—
And from the wall the whole hearth will divide,
Revealing now a torch-lit, secret hall
With spiderwebs and skulls—but stay thy fear,
For meddlers, when they plumb the hollow wall,
May enter, but will not soon reappear.
Now take this lanthorn, follow to the end—
O, yes, it flickers—drafty here, and chill,
Where anciently my ancestors would bend
Both men—and Other Things—to do their will,
And when you're done exploring hereabout,
Just knock, and I will come and let you out.

But press a quarter of
this shield of stone,
Good mistress, and this block
will roll aside;
Then pull this ring and chain--we're
quite alone--

And from this wall the whole hearth will divide,
Revealing now a torch-lit, secret hall
With spiderwebs and skulls --but stay thy fear;
For meddlers, when they plumb the hollow wall,
May enter, but will not soon re-appear.
Now take this lanthorn, follow to the end --
Oh, yes, it flickers; draughty here, and chill.

Where anciently my ancestors would bend
Both men --and other things-- to do their will.
And when you're done exploring hereabout,
Just knock, and I will come and let you out.

—Fred Phillips
Bensonhurst, Brooklyn, N.Y.
July 18, 1985

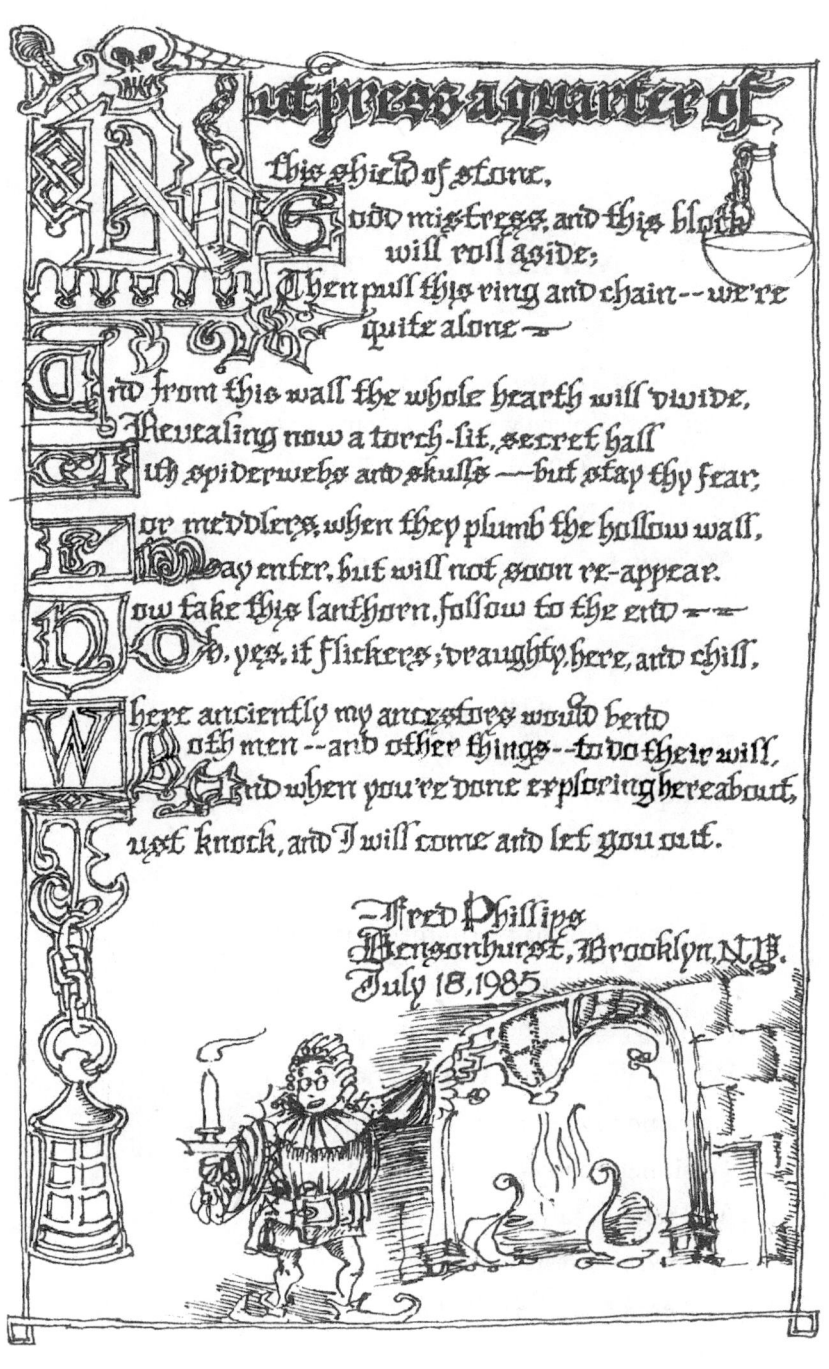

Master and Pupil

"The Road," he wrote, "goes ever on,
Back to the place where it began,
And I must follow if I can . . ."
Or sit, like Bilbo, 'neath his tree
And watch the passing company.
Two Dwarves, in dark clothes, travel-stained,
Whose caution silently restrained
The words from falling from their lips
The while they stopped for fellowship,
And quaffed my hospitality
From pewter-tankards made in Bree.
A Wizard came: I knew the type,
A long staff, broad-brimmed hat, and pipe;
In these adventures never surly
(At least, by no means, quite so early).
What rede he bore, I'll straightway tell:
He came to test my skill in spells;
To sit before my cozy hearth
And tell old tales of Middle-Earth.
I passed two tests, and yet another;
And ere he left he called me "brother."
He said in one month he'd return

Therewith the rest then I should learn.
I caught his sleeve and smiled: "My friend,
If you will but your patience lend,
I'll tell you all about your quest,
Since you have been my honoured guest.
Grave counsels bring you to the Elves
Who know in part your tale themselves.
The Shadow hath been overthrown,
And yet your work is far from done.
A fleet will sail from Western strands,
At Cirdan's wharves its host to land;
A horde of undefeated Orcs
Will give their broadswords desperate work.
In Egladil the horns will sound
A hundred feet above the ground;
And Moria's great drum will boom
To muster ranks from Khazad-Dum;
The earth will quake beneath their hooves
And wake the doves from peakèd roofs;
In all their counsels you will lead,
Well-mounted on the Eorling steed.

Well fitted are you, then, for war—
But all this you have heard before.
Once peace returns, you disappear
As though you were not needed here.
Now how are we to—by my troth!—
Be 'guardians' of Middle-Earth?
As fighters, Maiar swords are keen;
As mentors, few and far between!"
"I hope," he said, "you don't suppose
The best among our Order knows
The littlest point you're driving at!"
"Go to," quoth I, "and as for that
I know that you well understand
My meaning in the thing at hand.
If you had posted Watchers where
The smokes of Mordor choke the air,
We'd scarcely need to muster Elves
To do what we should do ourselves!"
He stroked his nether lip and frowned:
The fire made a popping sound.
"This is our portion: watch and wait,

Take counsel with the Good and Great;
Drive evil from the haunts of men
And back to Valimar again."
"If you fall ill, then what's to do?"
"My dear boy: why, I thought you knew!
You've passed your spells—now 'tis your turn
To show the world what you have learned.
Good luck! And, if you need our aid,
Just walk in moonlight in the glade,
And recite the ancient spell—
A Elbereth Gilthoniel!"

Paean to Duchess Ysabeau

For sixteen years the Tortoise in his shell
Hath lain in exile through the season's hues;
But age and illness do severely spell
The waning of his powers, wanting use.
One noble lady, kept in memory's hoard
Sustained him through those bleak and empty years,
Before her fairest face, beside her lord,
Evoked through bardic arts their joys and tears.
Ere Reaper come to his grim harvest bent
On adding Tortoises to his array,
Upon one final Quest is he now sent
To do her pleasure, his poor skills to play,
From Caledon to MacWeldon's Braes,
Cameron's fairest lady for to praise.

Der Brüder Unbekennt

There is a brother we have not yet met,
And I would clasp his hand in fellowship;
A friend in weather, be it dry or wet,
And such a messmate makes a mellow ship,
Who will attend in tourneys or at revels
And gladly bear a hand to clear the lists;
From whose good works fly unrepentant devils
Who know but wreaking chaos with their fists;
Whose courtesy were never less to aught,
But high and low alike must him esteem,
From whom the field of foes were dearly bought,
And maketh heavy labour nothing seem.
When he comes, ye need but say the word,
And I will proffer him my hand and sword.

There and Home Again

Mayhap 'twill be that I will go
Into the wild world and its roads
Some day, to visit those I know
And learn how they have borne their loads.

Past shining city will I wend,
Through sleepy hamlet, busy town,
Where past with present freely blends,
And pilgrims lay their burdens down.

With old friends, drain a pot full free,
Forgetting all my foolish fears,
And tell them what they've meant to me
Through all the long and lonely years.

'Neath shady greenwood tree I'll rest
And break my fast by tinkling stream,
To watch the sun sink in the West
And lie in peace awhile, and dream

Of faces frequenting my thought
Whom well I loved long in my youth;
My exile had been dearly bought
By ceaseless quest in search of truth.

And when my journey, done at last,
Leads home my footsteps to my door,
I'll try not to regret my past,
The wide world's roads to seek no more.

Omnes Spectatores Assentiant

(All witnesses agreeing)

When wit and beauty severally occur
In one so young, then sages keenly stare
And marvel at the gifts bestowed on her
That few can compass, yet that all declare
A gift divine, for as God gave her these,
So He the world in likewise guerdon gave
That she her world might unceasingly please
To render virtue unto all who crave.
The light she beareth through the darkest day,
What bard hath pow'r such excellence to sing,
Or sculptor craft, or mercator to weigh
What awe she starts in beggar or in king?
For voice mute falleth—so is stilled the pen—
Not soon will her like walk the Earth again.

Judgment

At last, Trebor, we are met eye to eye—
Thy transgressions are weighty in the scales;
And Justice, who is rarely known to fail
Hath thee in compass—seek not then to fly.
A trail of blood hath brought thee to this place
That offers thee no succour nor relief.
Thou wilt thy debt pay for this tale of grief
Which is thy sigil—nor will ye efface
The malformations if thy baleful deeds
Signal among the History of Men
That they pray that will never be again
Which now are stript of Time's concealing weeds.
Pray not, for heaven grants not thee its grace,
And Time will thy name from its Book erase.

Elrond and Celeglas:
A Chance Meeting between Two Theoretically Opposed Elvish Heralds

What brings you here to Imladris, Lord Celeglas?
We thought King Dagor on your lore relied?
He spends his time a-scriving 'fore his hourglass
And leaves me free to wander far and wide.
Do you recall the Herald-moot of Gil-Galad,
When you and I and others plied our skill?
He never could abide an ill-wrought ballad
Of which, when *you* had done, we'd had our fill!
You never mastered blazons worth a farthing!
You're a nitwit! You're outmoded! You're a prig!
You said 'twas right to blazon horses' bardings—
I'd *die* before I mounted such a rig!
Now how d'you explain a "voided annulet"
When annulets are voided as a type?
Since when is sand described as "quartz granulet"?
I never heard such nonsense in my life . . .
But when at Dagorlad the Noldor Star-Light
Bore Aiglos in the siege of Barad-dur,

To bring the Shadow down became then our fight—
You were right preux; herald you never were.
Of miruvor I'd quaff a horn right gladly
With thee, good Celeglas, who drains the bowls,
But if you would cease blazoning so badly,
Hie to the scroll-room and review the Rolls!

Misty Hills

Too long have these time-weathered heights prevailed
With endless ribs of lichen-covered stone
To hold their sway on things known and unknown
Where powers yet unseen by any failed.

The links of time beyond all human ken
Are welded fast where men are loath to fare,
And none who live know whether or e'en where
The pow'r that ruled may show itself again.

These tomes were writ that mystified the wise
By learned doctors who long lingered there,
Kindled by strange and unreasoning fear
That aeons since descended from the skies.
Few brave these hills, for few may understand
That they were once wrought by no human hand.

Then and Now

When Zeus o'er stellar chasms once held sway
A vernal panoply 'neath stellar glow,
'Twixt blue and yellow stretched its timbry way
To where the creatures of the wildwood go.
Of daylight and the darkness it knew naught,
But bordered meads where hosts in armour met
And strove 'neath brazen trumps and grimly fought
Wherewith their crimson shades are lingering yet.
Few mortals ever plumbed this haunted wood
O'er which the stars in neutral silence reigned,
Nor hath e'en Clio ever understood
Wherefore its earth so bloodily was stained.
Forfend, therefore, its nighted glades to tread,
And leave in peace the barrows of the dead.

The Visitors

They come but once or twice a year
As though I were still living here;
Their harps they softly strum and play
The rondels of a bygone day.

And when they leave, the silent night
Once more enshrouds my feeble light,
And I must wait, oft till next year,
Until my Visitors reappear.

How long can puny mortals wait
To greet such pilgrims at their gate?
I'd seek them in their hidden glades
Or bend my ear for seelie-rades.

But hither must abide content,
Be my heart ne'er so outward-bent.
I live, not here, but far and long,
A journey for an Elven-song.

A worker in a human hive—
How can I say "I am alive"?
For when I meditate, it seems
I am the happier in my dreams.

Second Thoughts

The sad-faced moon climbs slowly through the skies
And keeps a lucent course throughout the gloom
That veils Hecate, Mistress of the Wise,
Who know those Paths that lead men to their doom.
Scarce known since elder times to human ken
Who scorn the counsels sager folk bestow,
Not gleaned from those who are beheld as men
Who know strange truths that mortals seldom know.
Those Paths far from the haunts of those who live
And never followed in the light of day,
For few desire what they have to give,
And for the rest no prodigy can say
To what end such a course will surely lead,
Or whether there was ever any need.

Homage

Hard by these ancient oaks, in solitude,
Far from the markets and the broils of men,
There stands a votive stone that gives the wood
Its name: The March, long sung by lute and pen,
Through which once rode lords of a granite age
Whose deeds of high renown the minstrels sang,
That great and lesser essayed to engage
Whose echoes through these leafy shadows rang.
O, Pilgrim, hither rest thy dusty feet,
And know this sacred ground whereon ye stand;
For him for whom this stone were raised, 'twas meet,
Once passed this way the noble Count Jehan.

Tom Byro

We have long passed the Middle of the Way
Traversed by all who to our world are born,
Though what we have accomplished, who can say?
From the Book of Life a single leaf is torn.
Full many times our questing feet have found
Emporia that housed the printed word
The which we brought home on walls to surround,
Though seldom after was a mention heard.
Many years passed with families in tow;
To southern climes we wended to sojourn
Where thousands other pilgrims used to go
And risked beneath the sun their skins to burn.
What lies ahead from human ken's concealed,
In quiet earth some future day revealed.

Poojaree and Sheir-Khan: The Tale of the Priest and the Tiger

The Baghri Priest, man of the East, in fever long had lain
Upon his bed with fiery head and tormented by pain,
And when the man to the village ran with news that the Colonel's child
Had disappeared—by the Prophet's beard!—lost in the jungle wild.

A strange light came—in lambent flame, like a coal in the Baghri's eye,
And he raised his head and arose from bed with a horrid strangled cry;
"The Colonel-Sahib hath spoken of the Great Queen's rule of peace,
And it were shame to Allah's name that his child should feed the beasts!"

He broke their hold and plunged full bold into that verdant hell,
Where creeper-vine the trees entwined so deep no man could tell;
But the stricken priest was not the least of the jungle's denizens,
And with Allah's aid he soon had made a path for the Baghri men.

He slowed and listened; his countenance glistened; his heart beat hard and proud;
The thicket moved; its rustlings proved what stealth and craft allowed;
The bushes parted; his breath then started as the dread Sheir-Khan came through
And spying his foe he crouched full low, his prey now in full view;

But when he sprang a shamshir sang from the old man's rusty sheath
"Now taste, Sheir-Khan, the tooth of Man!" cried the fever-ridden priest;
And the great beast's claws, and his savage jaws the frail old body tore
As the old priest smote the great cat's throat, and both sank in their gore.

The soldiers found on higher ground the child as she lay asleep,
And the Baghri men found the priest again inert in a crimson heap;
And they bore their rede on a rapid steed to Raj and village abode,
And mourning-cries soon filled the skies o'er the length of the Grand Trunk Road.

The snare-drums rolled and the pipers bold took up their mournful dirge,
And the Colonel first, their arms reversed, upon the town converged;
Arrayed full-dress, the Regiment's best, their colours with bunting hung,
And stayed till the Sun in the West was done, and the mourners' paeans sung.

Behold! O stranger, braving the danger of tooth and fang and claw,
To bring the folk of sand and oak the light of the Rule of Law,
For the years are long, and still the song is sung at the foot of the wild,
How the Baghri Priest, man of the East, gave a life for the Colonel's child.

Many Happy Returns

'Tis said we are asleep, though open-eyed,
With daylight all about—belike 'tis so,
But just as long as we are dignified,
The Sages may say true—we do not know.
Your birthday is a joyful mark in time
To punctuate the year with song and glee—
May Fortune bide with you in every clime,
And may each one more joyful be to you.

Pivrarcha

There atop Pivrarcha's misty crown,
Where winds roar staves that Time has long forgot,
And crystal flakes are scarcely settled down
When up they whirl to dance (this were their lot);
And creeping stealthily upon the crags,
The cat with human face and covert snarl
Coils, ready to dismember into rags
Whoso his realm invades: bird, beast, or jarl;
Where Nature's voice is fell; where oft howl storms;
Where heroes fret their proofèd gyves to rend,
And straining, fail, and baffled, curse the Norns,
And long for brand to wield and bow to bend,
And think, betimes, in silent solitude
Of wight they knew in softer, gentler mood.

Rendezvous

We thank the Gods our brother once again
Foregathers with us, gladly to commune
O'er tea and rice, creating for my pen
A tale for those who are not yet immune
To joyful counsels, tales of wondrous deeds;
The glowing dreams of youth spring up anew,
For this was what the flagging spirit needs
The hope of hunting what we always knew
Would lead to wisdom. Thus, our hope renewed
Fuels our resolve to meet him once again,
To fashion a constructive interlude
Well worthy of remembrance by the pen.
If he by this needs no more to explain,
By all our lights, we have not lived in vain.

Hymn to Odin

Do thou, High One, deign to see
Here thy faithful kneel to thee;
Grant thy people's flocks increase,
In war triumph, gain in peace.
May our Wise Ones ever heed
Thy good counsel with all speed
And when we die, jarl or thrall,
Grant us feasting in Thy hall.

The Song of the Haqqim

The breath of buran is hot, my brothers,
It carries the stench of gore;
Forsake forever the yurts of thy mothers:
We ride once again to the War!

Hai! That wind is a hot wind
That before our vanguard blows;
For a thousand years, to the plain of Hind,
It hath blown from the Kush and its snows.

It blew before Jinghis the Kha-Khan,
Before Subotai it danced
As their hosts wielded their yataghans
Against the Livonian lance.

Who shall withstand the buran?
The bones of our dog-brothers lie
From Bekra to Kabul to Samarkand
As dark clouds fill the Eastern sky.

Ai, the storm-clouds rumble and lower
And the drawbridges close in the West;
While our hearth-fires shimmer and glower
Like the jewels on a Djinni's breast!

Hai! the jackals of Meridies have ranted
They have judged our warriors least;
Whereso are the horse-tails planted,
There rule the swords of the East!

From the West come the strawberry-coronets
With Miruvor on their breath,
Like a swarm of furious hornets
To sting the invader to death!

When his fields are smoke-blackened and salted
And the minstrels sing his name no more,
And the tide of his conquest has halted,
He will know upon whom he makes war!

Reminiscence

I only wish that I could find a place
With faded photograph of FDR,
Where I might be another friendly face—
A little tavern, or a smoky bar—
And there I'd nurse my drink and swap my tales,
All heedless of the clock upon the wall,
And wait until all time and patience fails
Until I have with longing heart told all.
It recks not if the barflies heed my word;
The tale's my own: let them heed or depart;
Who will remember aught that they had heard
Before I stand and finally depart?
And none will ever know where my tales start,
Save in the deepest recess of my heart.

A Dream of Faerie

In labyrinthine recess of my mind
Abides a lamp, the passions' every seat
That breathes its luminescence on the kind
Of thoughts that shun the market and the street.
Such walls of wonder compass it and glow,
Beset with gems to shame a dwarvish king
Upon a golden pedestal, below
A painted dome with mythic figuring.
The Fathers of the Elves have sojourned here;
To faerie-queens their cunning minstrels play'd
Of more than heart's desire, and that dear
And mindless dreaming, where strange worlds are made,
And this same Lamp of Wonders will I bring
Where I am bound, when minstrels cease to sing.

Orison to Ra

Memory cries with a voice of thunder,
"Behold the sun in autumn's air!"
People pass with eyes of wonder—
Ra hideth His face—and thou art there.

No day dieth save we our hands
Raise to the West, our hope to share
On land, on sea, on island sands—
"Behold, O Ra—for thou art there."

Man is a reed that Time devours,
And sorrow grants scant joys to share,
Yet in the gloom of silent hours,
Ra leaves His light—for thou art there!

Bedmates

A child of Bastet, Maya leaps
Upon the bed on which I sleep;
Her brother, Inca, nothing loath,
Leaps up to where they settle both.
I scratch behind my roommates' ears,
My Inca stretches, yawns, and peers,
His paws upon my blanket press,
A cordial gesture, I confess,
And settles down the while I turn
The pages from which I have learned
How many more tomes yet unread
In growing piles lie near my bed.
The word is that a cat is yet
A poet's most appropriate pet.
At Karnak in the Khem of old
Bast reigned serenely o'er her fold;
A member of a lesser grade
Dick Whittington his fortune made.
Happy he who keeps such friends
Long lonely days their task to mend,
And let us render thanks at last
For friendship from the Sons of Bast.

Reward

Whoever thought we would be drawn abroad
To risk the strains of traveling so far—
A feat that few would be moved to applaud,
Merely to place our footsteps where you are?
We clasp the hands of kindred spirits, those
Who walk our ways, and those who with us strive
To bring our widened circle to a close
And offer greater cause to be alive.
Of all the things that ever we have done,
Our visit crowns a life lived far from home,
And few had thought rewards like these were won
To offer substance unto hearts that roam,
But scarcely ever made such steadfast friends
Along a lifelong Path that never ends.

Meditation

As I sit here, nodding slightly
Over half a cup of tea,
While the sun outside so brightly
Tries in vain to locate me.

Thus does the Muse avoid me;
I search for rhymes in vain;
This once might have annoyed me,
And it may yet again.

In th' Almanack, Rebecca
Charles Stanford's lines repeats:
From Tuskegee to Mecca,
There are few nobler feats.

"Count that day lost," saith V. Stanford,
"Whose low descending sun
 Views from thy hand (or my hand)
 No worthy action done . . ."

A baby fed and cuddled,
To a wife, a kind word said;

The world rolls on, befuddled,
But you may raise your head.

'Tis brief, our span of living,
And small the deeds we do;
From loving and from giving
May our qualities accrue.

Ostrgard

In bygone times our valour were approved
By those whose rightful calling was the sword,
And we would not by idleness be moved,
But strive to earn the favour of our lord,
And them whose charge it were to raise a host
Would counsels give and take with honest folk
Who ever have despised the idler's toast:
Whose limbs were strong, whose hearts were made of oak.
But we have sadly fallen to decay—
We wield the table-knife and shun the blade,
And leadership in war is scant today;
Yet fighters are not born but must be made,
And will we pray that Seigneur Dieu may give
Our warriors hope, that Ostrgard may live.

The Wanderer's Lay

"It little recks," an ancient minstrel quoth
  Who ever plied the Road of Middle-Earth,
"How long o'er far-flung bosk and lea we fare,
  With ne'er at journey's end to fairly share
  With kindred spirits aught rede of our quest;
  With meat and song, nor seldom take our rest.
  Yet driven are my kith, with shouldered lyre,
  Within whose souls there glows an ancient fire
  That goads and spurs us from our native home
  Across the wide and windy world to roam . . .

"It recks not whether we be man or fay,
  For unlike other folk unwinds our day;
  For leagues we tread the never-ending Road
  And when the first star gleams, unstrap our load
  To take our ease within some crumbling inn,
  For at next cock-crow must our day begin,
  And once again we don our weathered cloak
  And inwardly a sacred name evoke:

"We never are to know a day of rest
But ever doomed to roam upon our quest.
Look now with mercy on Thy bardic sons
And let us lie near where the Greyflood runs;
Give us some pause, if that it be Thy will,
As sight of us recedes beyond the hill. . . .'"

Magister

A captive of the Past, the chamber stood
    In silence louder than a Titan's roar
That echoed further than a distant shore
    No longer where the shades of daemons brood.

The footfalls of the Mage no longer sound,
    Nor subtle odors from his cauldron rise,
Confounding those who see with human eyes
    Or kindle fear on this unhallowed ground.

None measure all the aeons that have passed
    Unending dawns and sunsets that are one
With vanished ages since Time had begun
    Until the mighty Magus breathed his last.

That fearful lightning now in silence lies,
    No longer servant of his enterprise.

To Jon Singer

I cannot take a chopstick in my hand
Without your image sitting at the board;
Too few are left who still can understand
The spirit of a fan in memory stored.
You are a guest at every Chinese feast,
Nor raise my cup of tea save "This to Jon,"
And every word of praise is but the least
That even my poor fancy dwells upon.
It recks not that your letters are so few—
I know you are so often on the go;
I write to say I daily think of you,
And that we miss you more than you can know.
I've said my piece—in time, you may just write,
And then, at long last, all will be all right.

On Returning from a Pennsic War

Long the lines of pikestaves trailing,
Dull the plod of mud-caked schoon;
Clouds like camels slowly sailing,
Bear upon their humps the moon.

Long the fires of battle smoulder,
Corpses decorate each hill;
Dirty rags on head and shoulder
Advertise the butcher's bill.

Gallant banner, tasselled golden,
Flaps in tatters from its staff;
Are we to the gods beholden,
Sowing wheat and reaping chaff?

O, that I should live, and living,
Bear a tale of grisly red,
God takes more than He is giving—
He receives what kings have led.

Does the will to conquest flourish?
Does the thirst for glory burn?
By defeat is History nourished . . .
O! When Will We Ever Learn?

To Derrick Hussey

The day you came to call upon a friend
Was one of several that you asked me down
To supper and your company to lend
Before you took the subway back to town.
Poor provender I made you with my rhymes,
Unworthy verse that never seems to cease;
A better way to while away the time
Would be to let you simply eat in peace.
An hour more pleasant seldom comes to mind
Than breaking bread at sundown with a friend;
A better evening scarcely could I find
Except the happy company you lend.
You should have better poems when you dine—
I think by now you may be used to mine.

Frederic the Silent
Held in Durance Vile by His Lady

Ah, wel me wot, I cry an parlous dole!
What musick wolde ye from an herte y-chayned?
Or wolde blyth balladrye from woefull soule,
That lang in solytude hath ben y-payned?
A byrd in cage doth bettre fredom wot
That I may gyf the here withal to tell,
Nor envie, O myn maistres all, myn lot,
To byde away from the doth mak myn Hell!
And pitee, prythee, for Swete Chrystes' love,
Betimes to me endyt somdel of thee,
And gyf swete rede, mynhert for to move,
That I need nat abjure Chevalerie!

Looking Backwards

Long years of exile have mine inner eye
Ne'er truly dimmed that once dwelt on the brave,
And brightened o'er pale hands lay azure skies,
Whil'st o'er our heads full lordly banners waved.
A joint of roasted meat once made good cheer,
Most truly in the fellowship of friends;
'Twas bootless if we water quaffed or beer—
Such soaring joys but seldom find their end.
Yet even now, my hairs grown spare and grey,
I still recall the grip of gleaming sword
With which my shield I bore the livelong day
To do the pleasure of my ducal lord.
Farewell to all, both leman and to thane—
The years have flown, but memories remain.

A Maiden's Song

My true love is no gallant knight,
Nor courtly squire of love's delight;
He hath no mercer's wealthy hire,
But what he hath all maids desire.

My true love, he hath sworn a vow
If God him grant, he'll not allow
That I should die, when all is said,
And take with me my maidenhead.

My father is a miller stout
Who doth at ten ells hit the clout;
And he hath sworn me to defend
My virtue to the bitter end.

My true love hath two prancing steeds
To serve a lover's weighty needs,
And he hath brought them round to me
That I with my true love might flee.

My true love of the nut-brown ale
Hath quaffed, and sooth is very pale;
Now I his horse's rein must lead
That we may fly with all due speed.

When my true love awakes at dawn,
He'll wish he never had been born,
Or that poor maidens he hath led
To win them of their maidenhead!

The Voyage of Randolph Carter

The dark and fearful sea had blown them far
Beyond those shores where mortals made their home,
Beneath a black and baleful brooding star
Whilst on their bow gleamed incandescent foam;
And o'er the giant cataract they fell,
Conjoin'd betwixt the force of Time and Space
To whither e'en the wisest could not tell,
Bereft as they were of the slightest grace.
Into that realm where daemon pipers play,
Where tones unknown to human ears resound
That drove their spirits long and far away,
Nor knew they whether to unhallowed ground—
And now his tale makes fevered shudders grip
Those who recall his boarding of that ship.

Again a Quest

Unloose the clasp to Earth that binds thy feet
And wend ye unto whither we are bound,
Where many hidden paths and errands meet
And thou shalt know the Road those pilgrims found
So long ago who bore the Ring to Doom.
The Shadow hath thee in its ruthless toils,
And thou must choose to languish there for aye,
Or join us in a Quest for greater spoils
And walk thenceforth beneath a brighter sky.
O, sister—there are glories yet unseen—
Who knows what fortune any day may bring?
Mayhap we Ring-smiths, when that we convene,
Will share the powers of a greater Ring!
Despite a tyrant's strength, his power or pelf,
What slave be free save that he free himself?

A Song of Fall

O, list and hear, ye merrie folk,
Now thou art gathered here,
For I will make eftsoons a talk
That thee will make good cheer.

The aires of day, and likewise night
Have colder grown in season;
King Winter's North Wind roars with might:
This is, in part, the reason.

Loath be we all to wander far
From homely hearth and cot
To seek the moon, wish on a star,
Were this alone our lot?

Well wrapt be we against the cold,
Dwell we on dell or hill;
For be we young, e'en were we old,
We feare to take a chill.

And on the Lord's Day at the Mass
We pray the spring return,
In hope that winter will soon pass,
And thus God's grace to earn.

The Launching of the *Glen Carrig*

With all the skill that human hands could shew
Its keel was laid, its towering masts arose;
A carven mermaid graced its vernal bow,
A sailor's token, denotating those
To Triton's mysteries their fortunes bound,
Their lives to hazard on the vasty deep
In which the mariners of yore had found
Those horrors, foes of waking and of sleep
Gusted on winds of malefic design.
No mortal power had been known to spawn
That of their cryptic sources shewed no sign
Since Earth had known its first matutinal dawn,
And none can fathom wherefore they had planned
To make themselves the enemies of man.

Dim Horizon

The wagon slowly rattled into town
In dead of night, the wee hours of the morn,
Its ancient, bearded driver with a frown
Pipe clenched in teeth, his features lined and worn.
Its lantern glowing with a golden gleam,
It told of roads that wound through distant ways,
And it reminded us of what we dream
When darkness hides the luster of our days.
A tale in Romany did he relate
While from the trough his dark steed drank his fill,
And those of us who heard can clearly state
The temperature had gradually grown chill,
And long before the lingering night had gone
We wondered whence this traveler had come.

From the Uncollected "Tales of an Old Tavern"

In the ancient, smoky tavern where the cut-purse slakes his thirst,
And the greedy merchant guzzles nut-brown ale until he bursts;
Where the serving-wench is buxom, and her favours all can buy,
Save the tall, grey-cloaked stranger with the black patch on his eye.

O'er the cobbles of the alley, ancient waggons groan and squeak,
And in one day our landlord sells enough wine for a week;
Hear the hiccoughs pipe to quarters, blend with staves of bawdy song
As the young rake stands and swallows—by the gods, but not for long!

Youthful swagger bends to Bacchus; Dionysus gives him voice;
Slams his mug down on the table, yells the spot is his by choice;
Gaffer greybeard like a statue, sits and ponders with a sigh,
But the old red glare of battle leaps forth from the one good eye!

Now the crowd like hounds a-scenting smells the blood where none has spilt;
Burly waterman must jostle six-foot Highlander in kilt;
Comrades who but just this moment pledged each other's lives in beer,
Grip their hilts with sullen grimace, growl and step back with a sneer.

Up stands Gaffer, tall and silent, grips his spear in knotty fist,
Sends it flicking like a snake's-tongue with a very vicious twist;
Oak and skull meet with a force like summer-lightning's fearsome roar,
Soon the fighting catches fire, figures swirl toward the door.

Bodies hurl and pitch and tumble (Saints preserve the weak or slow!)
Death waits leering for the fumble-thus above—and so below!
Meanwhile Gaffer is reseated, from the table lifts his mug;
To serving-wench he nods and beckons; bring him up another jug.

Gaffer's done now with his drinking; wipes the foam from off his beard,
And is curiously thinking thoughts that most men hold as weird;
Grips his spear and stands up, grinning—half the topers now are
    down—
This has been a fair beginning for a night out on the town!

Solitude

When all you've ever tried to do has paled
And there remains to you no fleeting hope;
Your every plan, both great and small, has failed,
And you no longer feel that you can cope;
When friends like morning dew on grasses fade,
And every heart is full of hope save yours,
And there be no more compacts to be made,
And yours is the condition life abhors;
When days feel leaden you must bear alone,
And save your conscience, none to whom to turn,
And in your breast your heart has turned to stone,
Nor is there aught left that you still can learn,
Just when you feel that all you've known must end,
There comes at last the handclasp of a friend.

We, the people of the Ancient and honourable **PICTISH FREE STATE** in solemn convocation convened, by this testament declare ourselves pledged in honour for the common defence of our most cherished and ancient liberties ✠ seeking neither dominion nor eminence among the free peoples of the world, but a wholesome and peaceful commerce in pursuit of our right and lawful occasions, do we commend our trust unto the gods of our fathers ✠

Given this day of Wednesday, being of June the fifth day in the year MCMLXXXV, at **RIVENDELL**

Fred Phillips made these signs

www.ingramcontent.com/pod-product-compliance
Lightning Source LLC
Chambersburg PA
CBHW071126090426
42736CB00012B/2020